D0295252

STEVENSON PUBLICATIONS LIMITED

This book is published to help raise funds
for **COMIC RELIEF** and a donation of
10% will be made from every copy sold.

First Published 1995.

ISBN 0 9526395 0 5

Printed in Great Britain by
Wace Burgess, Abingdon, Oxfordshire.

Published by
Stevenson Publications Limited
19 Wharfdale Road, London N1 9SB.

INTRODUCTION

By Ronnie Corbett

David had been at Primary School for less than two weeks. One evening he overheard his father, who had just caught his thumb in a door, shouting out,
"Oh God!"
David immediately rushed into the room and, ignoring his father's discomfort, stated,
"I know who God is!"
"Oh, do you David?" said Dad, regaining his composure.
"Yes, we learnt about him at school."
"Did you really? And who is he?"
"He's a really good man and he lives up there," replied David, pointing skyward.
"Does he? And what does he do?"
David then spent several minutes educating his father about some of God's wonderful creations and miraculous deeds.
"Well, that's fantastic David. Does God have any children?"
"Yes, he has a son."
"And what's his name?"
Looking pensive and after a moments pause David replied, "I think his name is Stuart!"

The above true story is related by the editor of this book (David's Dad) and it is the main reason why this book has come about. If this is typical of the kind of 'gem' that children can bring home from school, how many 'gems' are there overheard that remain in the classroom?

With the overwhelming cooperation of teachers throughout the country we have managed to put together some of the funniest stories and situations that have occurred in and around the classroom. Our thanks to them and, of course, to you for your contribution to COMIC RELIEF by buying this book.

Some of these stories come from what children have said, some from what they have written and some from what they have done. All of them are linked together by one fact...they were not intending to be funny, they just were!

So dip in and giggle as you pay tribute to the world's natural comedians - children.

Ronnie Corbett is currently host of the highly successful TVshow 'Small Talk'.

Text book stuff...

The cost of food and bus fairies goes up on budget day.

He travelled through an African in search of an orchid.

I had breakfast then fed the sheep with my father.

I'm going to plant potatoes in my cousin's house tonight.

If I work hard enough I could make a big prophet.

The ship got a toe from another ship.

"Your spelling's adrift, buoy!"

The only reason I go to church is for the sweets.

Two different types of clouds are cirrus and columbus.

I was watching 'Points of You' on T.V.

Writing about an incident with a snake...
The tense fear gushed up to the innermost centre of my ventricles.

In a lesson about the 1066 invasion one pupil wrote...
William the Conqueror's real name was "Norman."

My Ideal School - It would be good if we had a choice of food but at least we get salt and sometimes we get tomato sauce. Instead of milk I would like Pepsi and Miss Maclean.

The Great Britain was built by King Dom Brunel of Israel.

She took me to the swimming pool. I can swim on myself.

My favourite pop grope is Status Quo.

They got vaccination to control small-box.

We live in the Outer Hebriblies.

Middle age is probably the happiest time of a person's life. Women stop having periods, although men don't always appreciate it.

The aristocrazy are very rich.

My brother thinks the Royal family should be treaded like ordinary human beings.

One day I was out walking and, across the road, I saw a herd of trees.

One of the main industries in Lewis is Harris Tweet.

The sort of patient who should not be given anything to eat or drink is an unconscious one.

His dive was called a swallow dive because he swallowed a lot of water.

Sirloin is the upper and best part of a lion.

Written by a child who was starting to use a dictionary...
Candles are Christmas,
Candles are bright.
Candles are genital,
Candles are light.

In a support spelling group the following was written by one child...
Lloyd went home on his battered old dik.

The connection between bread and the peasants' revolt is that the peasants were made into bread.

"Would that be sliced or unsliced my Lord?"

THE FUNNY SIDE OF TEACHING

The following are interpretations of well known proverbs and sayings...

"Your head's in the clouds"
Child one: *You must be a giraffe!*
Child two: *The wind blew your head off your body.*

"A stitch in time saves nine"
Nine people had to drop out of the marathon because they had a stitch in their side.

"Grin and bear it"
Plant the grin. When it is ready, take it to the baker's. Take the bread home to the bears.
If you were unhappy and a big friendly bear came, he would make you laugh.

"A dark horse"
Child one: *A white horse that got sunburnt.*
Child two: *A horse in sunset.*

"Many hands make light work"
The electricity men come to fix the light when it's broken.

"Silence is golden"
You have to be quiet once you get gold.

"Time and tide wait for no man"
Two robbers were in a man's house. One of them tied the man and the other stole his clock.

"On the top rung"
The bell on the roof.

“Never say die”
Don't change the colour.

“Where there's a will there's a way”
Child one: *There's a footpath to Billy's house.*
Child two: *William weighs everything.*
Child three: *All the Wills in the world are clever. If you can't do something you can ask one of them how to do it.*

“Spare the rod and spoil the child”
Don’t let the child go fishing.

“Keep your chin up”
If Mummy was buttoning your top button you’d have to move your head upwards.

“Better late than never”
If you were better from being sick and late to a place you would be happy that you are there.

“Day in and day out”
If you were out playing with your friends and it started to rain you would have to go in and play in your bedroom.

“More haste, less speed”
If you go fast the police might come and get you.

“As weak as water”
If you are old you can’t swim.

“Down in the dumps”
Thrown in the bin.

What the teacher did...

It was a very snowy day and, before school, Dean had been walloped in the eye by a soggy snowball. It swelled up and became rather red. Unable to contact his parents, we kept him at school and periodically checked to see if he was surviving. Mid-afternoon Dean had forgotten the incident and was engrossed in building a 3-D model of The River Nile. Mindful of my responsibilities to his welfare, I asked him, "How's the eye, Dean?"
With a look of bewilderment on his face, you could see him internally searching for a sensible answer to what he thought he'd heard, moments later it hit him and with all seriousness he said, "Ho-de-ho, Sir!"

Peter Williams

It was the first time I had ever taught in reception class and I spent the first morning mopping up tears, keeping spirits up and toning some down. One tiny four year old interrupted at five minute intervals to ask when he could collect his 'present'. I attempted in vain to discover what on earth he meant. A toy left in the cloakroom? His school milk? Something in his coat pocket? All my guesses were met with irritated frustration.
All was revealed at lunchtime when one angry mother burst into the classroom demanding to know why her son's trousers were so soiled when he'd been asking to go for a 'present' all morning.

Janet Smith

At the beginning of the Autumn Term the usual flood of holiday photographs arrived for my perusal. At breaktime I leafed through some snapshots of a caravan holiday in Scarborough. My interest was suddenly aroused by poses of Mummy and Daddy in various states of undress and position draped across the caravan furniture. I returned the photos to one innocent child who admitted...
"No, Mummy doesn't know I've borrowed them, but I'm sure she wouldn't mind."
Needless to say, one set of parents were conspicuous by their absence for the rest of the academic year!

Janet Smith

Several years ago we had a teacher called Miss Hewes. At lunchtime everyone was in the staffroom and a knock came at the door...
"Have you seen Miss Hewes?" a voice cried,
"Pardon" replied the teacher,
"Have you seen Miss Hewes, please" (thinking politeness was needed),
"What do you mean?" replied the teacher,
"Have you seen Miss Hewes in the staffroom?"
"Don't be silly, boy, I can see them on your feet!" came the reply.

Neil Carline

Following a whole year of being a target for a constant stream of well intentioned practical jokes, aimed at me by my Year 9 English group, I decided one hot summer's morning, that the time had come for me to gain my revenge.
I arrived unusually early to the classroom for the first lesson

of the day and hid in a badly ventilated, walk-in cupboard, with the intention of, when the whole class had arrived, suddenly jumping out and shouting something at full volume.
As the seconds turned into minutes and the minutes turned into quarter of an hour, very few voices were audible in the classroom - and this was normally a very noisy class!
In any event, the hot water pipes in my 'hideaway' were now making me feel a bit sick and very uncomfortable and I was sweating quite badly!
Seizing the moment, with a mighty effort I burst open the cupboard doors, sprang-out and shouted ***"Wwwhhhaaaay"***... only to face a rather shocked and disturbed group of quite elderly exam moderators, sifting through some CDT coursework... my normal lesson had been moved to another classroom for that day!

Steve Foxhall

Two weeks into my first Headship I was determined to impress those around me with my ability to control all manner of problems thrown at me when the following incident brought me down to earth with a bump.
I was in my office with the Deputy Head discussing philosophies of education or some such important sounding issue (I was trying to impress you'll remember) when there was a knock on the door and a member of staff pushed in a child for me to 'deal with'.
Determined to show the Deputy how it should be done, and to give the boy a dressing down that he would never forget, I launched into him with a torrent of well chosen 'punishment centred' hot air. As I warmed to my task, wagging my finger

and pushing myself further back in my swivel chair, there was a loud crack and the chair collapsed. I found myself on my back, legs in the air with bits of chair all around. The Deputy was struggling to control mounting hysteria as I finished my speech from the floor ending with,
"And don't dare do it again!"
The boy didn't bat an eyelid but whispered, "Sorry" and quietly left the room leaving the Deputy Head on her knees, helpless with laughter.

Mark Gallacher

In the first PE lesson of the new term, one of the boys lost a grey sock. We searched everywhere but to no avail. Inspiration!
"Is your name in your sock?" I asked.
"I'll check this one." came the reply.
On checking, the boy found that he had both socks on one foot!

Chris Allen

A few weeks ago I was choosing teams for a rounders match. In order to decide who was to bat first I asked the following question...
"Finish off the name of this famous '70's supergroup... Emerson Lake and ?"
One of the team captains answered,
"Windermere!"

Chris Allen

OFSTED - An Inspector calls

Alice's mum advised Alice to be good during OFSTED.
"The teachers are very busy. They are having a stressful time getting everything ready. They are working very hard and being watched all the time."
"Huh!" said Alice, "That happens to us every day!"

Inspection time, one boy announced to his parents...
"The inspector inspected me eating my sandwiches!"

Picture the scene - me, a difficult class of very mixed ability upper juniors in the last week of my final teaching practise, my mentor observing, a SAWA for support and my Area tutor from college who had come to write my final profile.
We had been doing electricity in depth for ten weeks. The children were gathered on the carpet. Keen to show that they had grasped a lot and my questions were differentiated to include everyone, I asked a girl, "What's electrical in your home, Sarah?"
"My gas fire!" was the reply.

Influence of OFSTED? Overheard in class...
"Let's play Inspectors."

We felt rather harassed and somewhat demoralised towards the end of our inspection week. Year 2 had watched a video which prompted discussion on the word 'precious'. Comments were centred on value and possible antique value.
"Mrs Curnow."
"Yes, Amy"...
"You're precious."
I contemplated hugging the child on the spot... then she continued, "because you're old!"
The inspector smiled faintly.

Child age 6 talking to an inspector who had been inspecting the school for 2 or 3 days...
Child: "Please, Mr Richards, can I ask you a question?"
Mr. Richards, hesitantly, "Yes."
Child: "What do you do when you go to work?"

During School OFSTED Inspection Week...
Pupil to teacher: "Oh, Miss, I'm so tired."
Teacher: "Oh, why is that?"
Pupil: "I've been inspected ***three*** *times already this week!"*

Letters to the teacher...

Excused letter...
Dear Miss,
Please excuse Sandra being late. She was waiting for the bus at twenty to nine, but came back to use the toilet and missed it.

Comment a child wrote for her end of year report...
My Maths is O.K. and I think I am quit god at splelling.

A probationary teacher at our school very tactfully approached a pupil who had a hygiene problem and advised that her mother should wash her dress over the weekend, so that her class mates would stop making comments about the smell. The following letter was later received by the Headmaster...
Dear Headmaster,
Our Dolorez comes to school to be teached! Not smelt like a bloody daffodil!

Excused note given by a year 7 child...
Dear Miss Woe,
Please could Victoria be excused P.E. today as she has bruised her cock sick at the bottom of her back. Thank you.

Excused letter...
Dear Sir,
Derek was not too well yesterday he has to go to the treatment centre with his fingers.

"I'm afraid you son's got a severe case of Eyes, Mrs Higgs"

Excused letter...
Dear Sir,
Georgie had to go to the hospital yesterday with eyes and he was going mad with the toothache as well.

Excused letter...
I am very sorry John has not been to school as he has a bad complaint running to the toilet...

Excused letter...
Andrew was unable to draw a 'Space Man' as we have not got anything with a picture for him to copy.

Apology...
I shouldn't shout across the room because it is selfish and neglectic.

Letter from Pupil to Headmaster...
My sporting interests are in a number of fields.

Parent's letter to school...
Please don't force Sheila to take her helping of cabbage at school meals. She just brings it home every day stuffed into her socks!

"Teacher says you still have to have cabbage but you don't have to stuff it in your socks yourself."

Apology...
I laughed when I saw Adrian Philpott laughing at something someone had said. I heard part of what was said and when I saw Adrian laughing it made me laugh because laughing is infectious. I am sorry for laughing and it will not happen again.

Excused letter...
Dear Sir,
David has been home under the Doctor, as he got Excema from a swomp down the Moatfield. It all swelled up the Doctor gave him some cream to put on it, it is now healed but you can still see were he's had it also on his hands. It was not coughing and now he can put his shose on.

...and from the Teacher...

Letter (nearly) sent to Mr Patten, (then Secretary of State for Education)...

Dear Mr Patten,

I have recently been addressing myself to the problems of discipline in my class. I am writing to get your approval of my solution.

As you may know, the incidence of bad behaviour in schools is growing. I am well aware that this can be as minor a problem as whispering to a friend, or as severe as hiding the teacher's cup of tea. Knowing what degree of punishment to mete out has long been a headache for conscientious teachers like myself, but not any more. I have the answer.
I would like sturdy metal hooks fitted onto the wall of my classroom, about six feet from the ground. If any child misbehaves he can then immediately be suspended from a hook. In the case of a fight between two or more children, I would suggest the hooks being at least one metre apart. Further distance can be added for older children, depending on their swing capacity in a karate kick or their left hook, whichever is the greater.

I am hoping that this method will deter children sufficiently in Primary schools, as the obvious difficulties of punishing sixth formers with cranes from McAlpines might prove to be so exciting that I fear it might be sought after, rather than feared, but let us be positive. I'm sure that after the Infant level we will have eradicated the problem. Persistent behaviour problems could be hung straight up by their parents as they drop them off at school in the morning, and removed by them at the time they are normally picked up after school.

Packed lunches would have to be provided, of course, but the child could be hooked up wearing a satchel or back pack containing this.

My only concern is that these children will not be able to follow the full National Curriculum, although there is no reason why they should not be able to participate in classroom discussions. For P.E. and games, they could be transferred to hooks in the hall or on the outside of the school building.

I have even solved the problem of what to do with them while I am on playground duty. Until we can get something organised through the schools catalogue, I will adapt the school play costume rail, so that I can wheel them around the playground.

I can hear you breathing a sigh of relief as I finish. I know I will be hearing from you very soon.
Best wishes and keep trying to get it right.

Patricia Kirwan.

Put-down...
Shamsul is always keen to please in the classroom but does not really see his work as of primary importance.

End of term Mathematics report...
Helen not infrequently sets off on the wrong path but most often along no path at all.

Teacher's letter to parents...
Your child has been selected for cooking. Please send 50p towards the cost.

In conversation...

A small boy, lost in admiration at his teacher's green and tartan outfit, commented...
"Mrs Thomas, you look just like a bagpipe!"

On a swimming coach, one boy said to his teacher...
"If you had a real job, what would you do?"

Watching frogs in the pond, one boy asked the teacher...
"Mrs Lloyd, how does the frog get back in the egg?"

One girl brought her Ginn Maths to be marked. She had been learning how to draw up charts of sports matches. On the page, very neatly drawn, were four chairs and a table. The teacher checked why what appeared to be art work was in her maths book and she replied...
"Well, the question said draw a table for four players."

Teacher: "What does 'Royalty' mean?"
8 year old child: "Is it a special drink for Kings and Queens?"

Working on the theme 'Ourselves', one boy said...
"Skin keeps the blood and bones in!"

Teacher, Sequencing: "What comes first, the apple or the core?"
Boy's answer: "The sandwiches!"

Overheard in assembly...
"I've seen a rainbow."
"I saw one yesterday."
"I saw one tomorrow!"

One boy took his spelling worksheet home. Mum noticed he was writing all his words backwards. "Whatever are you doing?" she asked. The boy replied...
"Mrs Lloyd said we had to learn these backwards."

During one morning assembly the children had been singing 'He's Got The Whole World In His Hands'. At the end of the song the Deputy Head asked who had got the whole world in his hands. One of the more well read members of the school raised his hand and shouted...
"Charles Atlas, Miss!"

Teacher in reception class closely observing and talking about conkers. In the hope of getting the word 'conker' in another language...
"Has anyone got another name for this?" (Holding up a conker)
After much thought, a child replied...
"What about Mark?!"

Teacher to 9 year old...
"Edward VIII was the Duke of...?"
Child... "Hazard?"

Teacher: "Joe, what happens when a ducks feathers get dirty?"
Answer: "His mum would tell him off."

Teacher: “Does anybody know what this duck is?”
Child: “It's a Mallard.”
Teacher: “That's very clever, how did you know that?”
Child: “It's a pub in Richmond, init!”

Child holding out Poppy Day money...
“Miss, when are the puppets coming round?”

On being given a blank piece of paper...
“Do I have to do a margarine on it, Miss?”

During a lesson on the letter 'V'...
Teacher: “Who's the man who looks after animals?”
Child: “God.”

School teacher was asking the class to put their hands up if they could name any of the five senses. One child raised his hand...
“Armpits, Miss!”

5 year old Martin arrived at class one morning and announced that his daddy had gone to Dubai. His teacher offered to show him where it was on the globe and asked, “Has he gone via Turkey?”
“Oh no!” replied Martin, “He's gone on an aeroplane.”

Involving a child in it's own Education Plan...
Teacher: “Now, Billy, what have you got to improve next?”
Billy: “Spelling and lying!”

5 year old Edward was reciting the words of a Christmas carol to his mother and said,
"Away in a manger no crisp for a bed..."
"That's not right," said his mother.
"Oh yes it is!" replied Edward, "They hadn't got any crisps to swap for a bed so he had to lie in a manger!"

I was recently having to go to classes to remind the students to bring money in for a trip, no later than that Friday.
Two children put up their hands.
"I can't bring the money by Friday, Sir," said one child.
"And why not?" I asked.
"Sir, my mum has gone on holiday to Spain," came the reply.
"Very nice too. Well I must have it early next week," I replied as I moved on to the second pupil.
"Is there a problem?" I asked.
"I can't bring the money by Friday."
"Why not?"
"My dad's gone on holiday."
"Oh, and where has he gone?"
"He's gone to Spain with his mum!"
I was lost for a reply.

After a course on Sex Education one child came to the teacher in a state of great anxiety...
"Do we **have** to have sex, Sir?"

Teacher: "You haven't written the answers to the sums."
Pupil: "You didn't put any answers on the board."

Returning to seat to correct a mistake...
"I thought that was wrong because I did it without my brains."

Child to dinner lady...
"Did you have Mussolini pudding when you were at school?"

Overheard in class...
"I've never been to the beach. I've only been to the seaside."

Whilst discussing an outbreak of measles in the class, one child was heard to say...
"One day I had chicken pops!"

Overheard in the dinner queue...
"He's not allowed in the dinner hall. He's not canteened!"

In a school general knowledge quiz, a group of first years were asked...
"What is unusual about Hong Kong airport?"
Eager to impress, one young lad pressed the bell and blurted out,
"Is it underground?"

End of Road Safety talk with a group if inner city Junior children...
Question: "Now then, where is the safest place to cross the road?"
Answer: "Bangladesh."

I was hearing the news of a class of Reception children aged 5. Amongst them was a pair of identical twins, one of whom announced that their black cat had died at the weekend. The other twin promptly said...
"Yes, and he's gone to heaven now," to which I replied,
"and what was your cat's name?"
"Satan!" came the reply.

I was busy at my desk one Eastertime, stapling a pre-coloured net to create an Easter basket which could later hold the mini Easter eggs which the 'Easter Bunny' would bring. A queue was beginning to form, and one child turned to another and remarked...
"She's going to use her stabilisers on us in a minute!"

Two infants were looking at a globe. One was pointing at various places, saying,
"There's Norway, Sweden, and that's Iceland." The other then said,
"Oh yeah! My mum goes there every Friday night!"

1st year Sound-Sense lesson...
Teacher: "Who can give me a word with the 'ss' sound in it?"
Pupil: "It..is..pissing..down..with..rain!"

Whilst studying ancient Egyptians in Year 4 class, two girls came up and said they knew a song about the Egyptians and began to sing, in perfect harmony...
"Pharoah Jacques, Pharoah Jacques..."

1st Year girl...
"I hope I don't catch ignorance, it said on the telly you can die of ignorance!"

Embarrassed...
"Darren! Take that out of your mouth this instant and put it in the bin! What is it?"
"My brace, Miss."

Overheard in the school corridor...
"I haven't done any work all week except in RE, and that was a miracle."

Educational Psychologist to teacher...
"He isn't a thief, but he has been found with a number of missing things in his possession."

Headteacher's speech...
"I will know when I've said enough when you stop looking at your watches and begin shaking them."

Headteacher's speech...
"I enjoy talking to people who are intelligent, caring and sensitive, and I don't really mind talking to a group like yourselves."

Headteacher's speech...
"The only clothes his parents could afford were those they bought from the Army and Navy Stores. They were wonderful quality but he found it a hell of an embarrassment going to school dressed as a Japanese Admiral."

One lad at school, a keen musician, was constantly telling me about this wonderful group he'd discovered called 'Jimmy Curry'. Not wanting to appear too old I pressed him to bring in this marvellous album only to find that Jimmy Curry was in fact 'Jamiroquai'.

"I was so frightened my head was in my mouth."

11 year old boy had researched into the life of St. Paul and began his presentation to the class...
"St. Paul was famous for spreading the message of Christianity throughout the Genitals."

Jesus cured the 10 leopards.

Testing times...

Exam Question: What changes happen to your body as you age?
Answer: When you get old, so do your bowels and you can get intercontinental.

Exam Question: What guarantees may mortgage companies insist on?
Answer: They'll insist you're well-endowed if you're buying a house.

Exam Question: Which is the nearest French port to Dover?
Answer: Calais - unless you go by aeroplane.

Exam Question: How should you start to treat patients suffering from shock?
Answer: Rape them in blankets.

Exam Question: What is a co-operative?
Answer: It's a kind of shop that's not as dear as places like Marks and Spencer.

Exam Question: How important are elections to a democratic world?
Answer: Sex can only happen when a male gets an election.

Exam Question: What was the fate of Anne Boleyn?
Answer: She was condomed to death.

Exam Question: Anthropology is the study of what?
Answer: Ants.

Exam Question: If the letters MW appear on a radio, what does it mean?
Answer: Don't play it on top of the microwave.

Exam Question:What caused the Depression of the Thirties ?
Answer: Lots of people being depressed because they didn't have much money.

Exam Question: What are people from Denmark called?
Answer: Dames.

Exam Question: By 1932, how far had Adolph Hitler got towards his aim of leading Germany?
Answer: He was a respiring politician.

Exam Question: How did decimalisation alter currency in the UK when it was introduced in 1971?
Answer: Before that, there were 16 ounces to one pound sterling.

Exam Question: What is the correct name for the method of providing water for crops in dry areas?
Answer: Irritation.

Exam Question: What is the essential difference between an annual and a bi-annual plant?
Answer: An annual is the name given to a plant which dies every year. Bi-annuals only die once.

Exam Question: What is Economics the study of?
Answer: Economic things.

Exam Question: What are your plans for the future?
Answer: If I pass my exams, I want to go into bonking.

Exam Question: What is artificial respiration commonly known as?
Answer: The kiss of death.

Exam Question: Chow mein is a popular Chinese dish. Name some others.
Answer: Kebabs and also chips with curry sauce.

When asked to explain the connection between miles and kilometres, one pupil replied...
"Miles measure the distance from A to B, with kilometres it's the other way round!"

"It's 3 miles in that direction or 5 kilometres if we walk backwards!"

Exam Question: What is a liberator?
Answer: A thing women buy in naughty shops.

Exam Question: Give an example of unacceptable food hygiene.
Answer: If you find a bird dropping on a table, it's not alright to eat.

"Waiter - there's a bird dropping in my soup!"

Exam Question: What is the currency currently used in Copenhagen?
Answer: The Denmark.

Exam Question: What is most important in a letter applying for a job?
Answer: You must spell the words write.

Exam Question: What do the letters HRH stand for?
Answer: Duke of Edinburgh.

Exam Question: Who is the patron saint of travelling?
Answer: St. Pancras.

Exam Question: Give an example of a white lie.
Answer: My library book was late once because I couldn't get down there through the flue.

Exam Question: What were the three major causes of the American Civil War?
Answer: a) Indians b) Hot weather c) Arguing.

Exam Question: What is Charles Darwin best known for?
Answer: His book, The Origin of Speeches.

Exam Question: Explain the social injustices facing children during Victorian times.
Answer: Little ones had to go up chimneys to get their pocket money.

Exam Question: Why do trees lose their leaves in Autumn?
Answer: To grow cabbages.

Question: “What do birds of prey use to catch their food? Here’s a hint, it begins with 'T'.”
Answer: “Testicles.”

Question: “In Victorian times poor people used to go to pawn shops. Can anyone tell me what a pawn shop is?”
Answer: “It's where you get dirty books and magazines.”

Question on secondary school passport:
What's your greatest fear?
Answer: Being frightened!

Exam Answer:
Red, pink, orange and flamingo are the colours of the rectum.

Exam Answer: I've said goodbye to my boyhood, now I'm looking forward to my adultery.

Exam Answer: Monotony means being married to the same person for all of your life.

Exam Answer: Jesus healed people with very bad illnesses; like the widow of Nairn's son; he was so ill he was dead.

Exam Answer:
When you are around 15 and have a baby, you could do it physically, but not mentally. It is best to have sexual intercourse when you are around 20 or over and when you have settled in. It is the busiest time of your life.

Year 9 History Exam Answer:
the Queen was Marryanne Twanet.

Year 9 History Exam Answer:
Bias means overagjagderating.

Question on a Rural Science Exam Paper...
What steps would you take to eliminate garden pests?
Answer: The steps what I would take would be very heavy ones.

Notice board...

Advertisement for teacher...

FULL TIME TEACHER OF MATHEMATICS WITH GAMES TO TEACH FOR G.C.E. 'O' LEVELS.... THE APPLICANT SHOULD BE A CONVICTED CHRISTIAN.

Dining Room request of students...

After your meal, please return your used food.

Excerpt from a local paper...

The school is presently situated on about five acres of steep land, and has 445 children on the roll.

School sign...

SCHOOL CHAPEL. NOT TO BE TAKEN AWAY.

Notice in a Norfolk school...

WILL THE INDIVIDUAL WHO BORROWED A LADDER FROM THE CARETAKER LAST MONTH KINDLY RETURN SAME IMMEDIATELY, OTHERWISE FURTHER STEPS WILL BE TAKEN.

Excerpt from the Kent Messenger...

Sir Roger Manwood's Grammar School, Sandwich, founded in 1563, will go educational in September next year.

Advertisement...

Sex Education : Who's responsible?
Please write for further details to ROSE.

Notice which appeared in a North East school...

QUIET, PLEASE. EXAM IN PROGRESS.
DO NOT PASS.

School notice...

NO EXIT FOR BOYS.
EXCEPT FOR DISPOSAL OR RUBBISH.

Recruitment advertisement...

WANTED IN JANUARY - EXPERIENCED MAN TO TAKE ENTIRE RESPONSIBILITY FOR THE LOWEST FORM OF BOYS.

Recruitment advertisement...

QUALIFIED TEACHER OF THE DEAD
REQUIRED AT THIS SCHOOL.

Excerpt from the Trent and Harrow Recorder...

Pupils from Earlsmede First and Middle Schools in South Harrow have collected seven sacks of grans for emergency relief in Africa.

Working parts...

Class 2 of Hardy Memorial Primary School were learning about anatomy and were asked to describe the functions of various parts of the body...

Scalp
Helps to keep your skin in place.

Skull
It keeps your head hard.

Radius
It's a radio in the body that makes you talk.

Pelvis
Part of the body that makes you sing. It helps your teeth stay in when they are biting something hard.

Diaphragm
It makes you hungry if you are on a diet.

Larynx
Keeps the ink for the appendix.

Liver
It checks your food out so there are no bad bits in it.

Sternum
It stirs your blood.

Fibula
Helps you not to say a bad word.

Pancreas
Fries pancakes.

Spleen
Sparks coming from the pancreas.

Appendix
A pen in the body drawing blood on your bones.

Vocal Chords
They are leads to plug into your tummy.

Kidneys
They have to be careful not to run and fall and cut their kid knees.

Tonsils
Help you to grow more teeth when they come out.

Abdomen
Helps their body grow and not get fat when you eat your sweets.

Upon closer examination...

Question: Who lives in Turkey?
Answer: Turkingtons.

Question: Why do fish have scales?
Answer: To weigh themselves.

Question: What is the first book of the Bible called?
Answer: Jennifer.

Question: Who is Prince Charles?
Answer: The Conqueror.

Question: What is a pomegranate?
Answer: A granny goose.

Question: Why has a lion got a mane?
Answer: Because he doesn't shave.

Question: What is a vote?
Answer: A van that goes on water.

Question: Where does Prince Phillip live?
Answer: In the Tower of London.

Question: What is an eyrie?
Answer: An insect with five arms and six legs.

Question: Who gets an engagement ring?
Answer: A person who is love sick and can't eat well.

Exam Question: What was life like in the First World War trenches?
Answer: It was OK when soldiers sang songs like Anyone Who Had A Heart to keep up their spirits.

Exam Question: People who suffer from insomnia are called what?
Answer: Insomniaphobiacs.

Exam Question: What is an artist?
Answer: A man who doesn't go over the edges when he paints his picture.

Exam Question: Why do roosters crow?
Answer: Because they have laid an egg!

Exam Question: What is the best way to protect crops from storms?
Answer: By planting trees. A 60ft tree can break wind for 300 yards.

Exam Question: What makes an aeroplane fly?
Answer: Jet petrol.

Exam Question: For what was Stradivarius famous?
Answer: For discovering the upper layer of the atmosphere.

Exam Question: Why is one of composer Handel's best-known works called Water Music?
Answer: Because he lived on an island.

Exam Question: What are the major symptoms associated with VD?
Answer: Sufferers from VD may get an inflammable penis.

Exam Question: What form of verse best describes Mary Had A Little Lamb and Little jack Horner?
Answer: Mercenary rhymes.

Exam Question: Who do you expect to see with a mortar board?
Answer: A bricklayers mate so he keeps the bricklayer in bricks.

Exam Question: What is the correct name for my father's father?
Answer: George.

Question: What rights do you have if you are sold out-of-date food?
Answer: You can always bring it up in the managers office.

Question: What problems may arise through water on inside walls?
Answer: They may be condescending.

Question:For how long should you boil a size 3 egg?
Answer: For no longer than four hours.

Question: Where did the UK get 95 per cent of its lamb from before we joined the EC?
Answer: Lamb farms.

Question: What's the capital of India?
Answer: I.

Exam Question: What is the function of antibodies?
Answer: Antibodies are organisations in dispute with people.

Exam Question: What is the major advantage of passing all your exams?
Answer: If you pass all your exams, you're certified.

Miscellaneous misnomers...

A fifteen year old girl confiding to a sympathetic teacher about her worries of inheriting her mothers illness, said "Cos, you know, Miss, it's genitals!"

12 year old boy on school outing, delayed in school coach by road-works on the way home, read the roadside notice which read 'Delays possible 'till June'. It being then February the boy protested,
"I'm not staying on this road in this coach until June!"

"Oh no it doesn't!"

Year 7 child in Biology lesson, proud to use newly learned vocabulary...
"The sea is full of orgasms."

Year 8 boy said that he felt faint in school assembly and that he had "nearly passed away."

An 8 year old boy being shown some Archaeological treasures, said...
"I like this one. It's from the Tudor period when King Henry VIII was on the 'phone!"

THE FUNNY SIDE OF TEACHING

A 10 year old boy was being told how pleased his teacher was with his work...
"And his vocabulary and comprehension are very good."
The boy asked,
"What's comprehension?"

A 4 year old boy running round the corner of the infant school building in the rain shrieked...
"That's a silly place to put a puddle!"

A 4 year old boy was talking about the children in his class at school...
"And there are two Alex-es, Alex Hinton and Alex Andra!"

3 - 4 year olds in playgroup, prior to singing a song about head, hands, feet etc...
"What is your head for?"
"Nodding!"
"What is your mouth for?"
"Eating!"
"What is your nose for?"
One bright 4 year old called out, "Picking!"

A 9 year old boy, being given an explanation about Christmas and how Jesus tried to teach us to be good people, thought for a while and then said...
"Yes, but he didn't teach me or Aaron Andrews very well, did he?"

On wishing a member of the Craft Department Staff well on his forthcoming wedding, the Deputy Head, at the conclusion of his speech, said...
"We wish you every happiness, and an easy passage."
He wondered why there followed a deathly silence before an uncontrolled eruption of tittering.

A teacher, reading a book aloud to a class, checked on their understanding. She asked...
"What does 'belated regrets' mean?"
An 8 year old boy replied...
"Well, if I killed myself, then I'd regret it!"

On a French trip pupil asks...
"How do you say Merci in French, Sir?"

From an enquiring girl aged 5, travelling past a cemetery and spotting the crosses...
"What are those Jesus things?"
"That's where people's bodies are buried when they have died."
After a decent interval came the supplementary question...
"But where do they put the heads?"

An 8 year old boy proudly told his parents that he is now doing graph work at school...
"What's it on, Son?" asked his father,
"On squared paper!" he replied.

A four and a half year old child being asked what work he had done on his first day at school said...
"Mostly put away the toys the teacher had been playing with."

Conversation...
"You don't know nothing, you don't."
Offended response:
"I ***do*** know nothing!"

Two infants rather timidly came into my junior class, walked up to my desk and one of them whispered,
"Please can Mrs Crosby have some bleeding paper?"
"Sorry. I haven't got any!" I replied. They went away.
Later I saw the teacher concerned who said,
"By the way, what did the two I sent to you ask for?" I told her and she replied,
"Oh! I sent them to you for blotting paper!"

From the school book...

Year 2 English lesson...
"Wives generally hunt in packs."

Year 2 English lesson...
"An inscription is something you get from a doctor."

As part of an essay answer in a History exam, a year 10 pupil at my Grammar school wrote...
... and Sir Francis Drake circumcised the World, with forty-foot clippers.

Written by one pupil in RE lesson...
Our father who ain't in heaven, hollow be thy name.

As part of an essay on moral issues, one child wrote...
Euthanasia ends life unnaturally, but it does make you feel better.

In a lesson about Islam and Ramadan, without any qualification, one pupil wrote...
Muslims are only allowed to eat in the dark.

In a 3rd year science class on 'Bridges', one pupil wrote...
Brides are one of man's most ancient and most important inventions.

Quote from year 5 language book...
I was falling and falling then I managed to grab hold of a giant prick but then it snapped and I kept falling again.

The snot of a swordfish is 6 ft long.

In response to the following test paper...

FIRST YEAR ENGLISH ESSAY EXAMINATION

Write an essay or story on one of the following topics:

1. Write about a book you have read in school. Be sure to name the book and say why you liked or disliked it.
2. Write a story which begins: "Everything went wrong from the moment I got out of bed..."
3. Write an account of one thing that has happened in your life that you will remember for the rest of your life.

Marks will be given for neatness, paragraphing, correct spelling and punctuation so take care.

...a slight misunderstanding resulted and this delightful story was submitted...

Mark will be given for neatness.

One day Mark went to school. He had to wright a story and when he writ it it was not neat. So the teacher said go and do it a gain. So after school he went home and he was practise doing his writing.

Mark come in to school in the morning. He started doing his writing and the teacher come over and said that is exlent he was copying out of a book he got given a prize, and it was a book called chip and chew pen.

Mark was made up and he started to wright bookes. His mother said that they will go on holiday.

When the last monarch died, it took six men to carry the royal beer through the Royal borough.

Written as part of a short story...
My dad used bicks wen he bit his arse.
(It was later explained that the child had meant...
My dad used bricks when he built his house.)

4th year moral education...
Adultery means you don't fall into other peoples arms, you must keep to one person only.

We got a cup for the best bread sheep.

10 year old writing about Winston Churchill...
When he left Sandhurst he joined the 21st Letchers.

In Russia the money they use is called rubbles.

A child in a biology class wrote...
Some of the things we use are made from dead pants.

Quote from history exam...
By 1800 vaccination against small-pox was being quite wildly used.

I had introduced the idea of big moral issues concerning life and death. As it was near the end of the lesson I explained what topics we would be looking at in more detail in the weeks ahead. For homework the pupils had to write an introduction paragraph for their books.
One pupil wrote a long section about the 'Youth in Asia'. It took some time for me to realise my mistake. I had spoken about the issues, but had never written the words on the board. So the issue of 'euthanasia' had taken on a whole new meaning!

He finished the job in a phew minutes.

Questions, Questions, Questions...

Question: What is the most expensive car one can buy?
Answer: A Maestro, because my daddy has one.

Question: Why do ducks have webbed feet?
Answer: Spiders make webs under their feet.

Question: Why is the sea salty?
Answer: The workmen who built the seaside put salt in the sea.

Question: What is an astronaut?
Answer: A knot that you tie with a string.

Question: Who is Margaret Thatcher?
Answer: A woman who goes on the news at night.

Question: When is the six o'clock news on the radio?
Answer: Five o'clock.

Question: Why do somc men grow beards?
Answer: They don't want anybody to kiss them.

Question: What is a cowslip?
Answer: A banana skin.

Question: What makes the most noise?
Answer: The biggest mouth.

Question: What is a parsnip?
Answer: A carrots wife.

Question: What is a psychologist?
Answer: A man who always rides a bike.

Question: What is a politician?
Child 1 answer: A man who goes round polishing everything.
Child 2 answer: A man that sells tissues.
Child 3 answer: A man that starts riots.

Question: Where do dates grow?
Answer: On a calendar.

Question: What is a millionaire?
Answer: A house that's got wings.

Question: What did Henry VIII want more than anything?
Answer: To marry Elizabeth I.

Question: How have penguins adapted themselves to a life in the ocean?
Answer: Chocolate Biscuit.

Year 7 maths paper...
Question: What is a menu?
Answer: Proncock Tale.

Test paper: Use 'bought' in a sentence...
Answer:My mum bought a three pea sweet.

Year 9 line of poetry...
There was a kipper swimming by.

Year 5/6 homework question: What does transparent mean?
Answer: When your parent has to travel.

Geography Exam paper...
Question: Give reasons why some countries have a higher birth rate than others.
Answer: It's because of the hospitality.

Question: Name any of the benefits of introducing the N.H.S.
Answer: It helped improve the mortality rate.

History paper year 10...
Question: Why were the Roman Legions considered a formidable fighting force?
Answer: Because when in battle they held their scrotums above their heads to protect them from flying arrows!
(Note: The Latin word for shield is SCUTUM)

Question: A bag has 8 lettered balls in it. What are my chances of pulling out an H?
Answer: Nobody ever wins these sort of contests!

Question: Fill in the missing word with the opposite of the word underlined.
'Two men were innocent INNOCENT, but one was _____.
Answer: Married!

Question: 20% of boys wear patterned socks. 20% of girls wear patterned socks. There are 35 boys and 40 girls. Who wears the most patterned socks and how many are there?
Answer: The girls...boys who wear patterned socks aren't cool.

Exam Question: What stood Henry VIII apart from all other English Kings?
Answer: He was the fattest human being of all time.

Question: The table shows that breeding rabbits for meat production is much more cost efficient than breeding bullocks. Give one reason why rabbits are not as popular as table meat.
Answer: You get much more meat on a bollock.

Exam Question: What is the major food intake of the people of Greenland?
Answer: Eskimos.

Exam Question: What does migration mean?
Answer: It's a headache that birds get when they fly south for the winter.

Exam Question: What was Leonardo da Vinci's major claim to fame?
Answer: Sailing the Mona Lisa round the world.

"Well, you know what they say - any port-rait in a storm!"

And finally...

During a suspected gas leak in a classroom, the teacher warned the class to be careful stating that gas tended to collect in pockets, whereupon the entire class started to empty their jacket and trouser pockets!

An A-Level Physics candidate, when asked to discuss 'off-peak electricity' explained that it was electricity which had been examined at the power station and found to be below standard. This was sold off cheaply in the evenings when people don't use so much!

At a parents' evening...
Parent: "How's he getting on then?"
Teacher: "I'm really pleased with his reading, but I'm still worried about his spelling and punctuation."
Parent: "Punctuation? I don't know what time he gets here, but he leaves our house at 8.30 every morning!"

Acknowledgements

We have made every effort to ensure that the material in this book has been credited and special thanks are made to the following:

Contributors

J.L. Abraham, Chris Allen, Avril Joy Banting, Stephen Bishop, Gareth Burnell, Stephen Cairns, Ian Carson, Jane Chesters, R. Curnow, Stephen Edgell, H.M. Fiddes, Alan Goodwin, June Griffith, David E Hanson, Mike Heath, Audrey Henderson, E.A. Higgins, Irene Hindley, M. Hornby, Glenys Huntington, Alan Jackson, S.A. Jarvis, Connie Johnstone, Patricia Kirwan, Alasdair MacLeod, Malcolm Moffatt, Cathy Parkinson, Janis Pickwick, John L. Raybould, Naomi Richardson, Steve Riches from *Yes* magazine, J.C Ridgley, C. Ryan, Harry Saunders, P.A. Savage, Jan Self, V. Shanley, Janet Smith, Gill Woe, R. Woolridge, C.J. Wright, Peter Young.
Thanks also to the staff at Alexandra Park Infant School.

Cartoonists

Paul Cemmick, Allan Davies, Pete Dredge, Noel Ford, Martin Honeysett, Tony Husband, Charles Jaffé, Matt, Fran Orford, Max Steiger, Colin Taylor, Nigel Thomas, Geoff Thompson, Pete Williams.

Cover photograph taken for 'Small Talk' and reproduced with kind permission of
Reg Grundy Productions GB Ltd.

Cover Illustration by John Richardson,
Richardson Studios, Cleveland Lodge,
45 Cleveland Terrace, Darlington DL3 7HD.